GW00793054

# Ocean

# Ocean

## Neil Azevedo

With a Foreword by
Richard Howard

Grove Press
*New York*

*Published simultaneously in Canada*
*Printed in the United States of America*

FIRST EDITION

Library of Congress Cataloging-in-Publication Data
Azevedo, Neil.
    Ocean / Neil Azevedo ; with a foreword by
Richard Howard.— 1st ed.
        p. cm.
    ISBN 0-8021-4196-X
    I. Title.

    PS3601.Z485O28 2005
    811'.6—dc22

                                    2004060940

Grove Press
an imprint of Grove/Atlantic, Inc.
841 Broadway
New York, NY 10003

05  06  07  08  09   10 9 8 7 6 5 4 3 2 1

# Acknowledgments

Grateful ackowledgment goes out to the following magazines where these poems first appeared, sometimes in slightly different forms:

*The Antioch Review:* "Snake"; *Big City Lit:* 'A Boy' and 'From the Crowd' from "Witness"; *Cimarron Review:* "Compunctio Cordis" and "Olivia's Bellybutton"; *Drunken Boat* (drunkenboat.com): "Supplicium"; *First Things:* 'Annas,' 'Barabbas,' 'Pontius Pilate,' 'Simon of Cyrene' 'Joseph of Arimathea,' and 'Nicodemus' from "Witness"; *Image:* 'Judas Iscariot,' 'Gestas,' and 'Three Marys' from "Witness"; *The Journal:* 'Peter' and 'A Soldier' from "Witness"; *LIT:* "Owen" and "St. Mary Magdalene"; *The Notre Dame Review:* "The Bearded Seal"; *The New Criterion:* "Animi Cruciatus" and "Marco Polo"; *The Paris Review:* "The Black Angel," "Caspar Hauser Songs," "Discarded Nude," "From the Hat," and "Stray"; *Prairie Schooner:* "Bad Boy"; *Shade:* "St. Maria-Goretti," "St. Dymphna," and "Ocean"; *The Western Humanities Review:* "For Myles."

"Caspar Hauser Songs" won the 1998 Bernard F. Conners Prize from *The Paris Review.*

One can't possibly thank everyone . . . but one can try: of course my mother, Karen; father, Bill; grandfather, Ramiro; brothers, Steve and Mike; my children, Myles, Owen, and Olivia; and their mother, Holly. The inexhaustible and lovely Richard Howard, who teaches me everything; Art Homer and Richard Duggin for teaching me everything first. Herb Liebowitz, Lucie Brock-Broido, Henri Cole, Marie Howe, and the brilliant Alfred Corn. Steve Oakman, Dianne Stannish, Paul Winner, Nicole LeClerc, and Evetta Andersson. Erin Belieu and Susan Aizenberg. James Raimes and George Plimpton for my jobs . . . and Jonathon Galassi, Bill Wadsworth, and Steve Riggio for helping me along. Fr. Tucker and Fr. Rafferty. Dan Kunitz, Ben Downing, David Yezzi, John Foy, David Larzelere, Ravi Shankar, and the awe-inspiring Max Watman. Scott Roth, Jim Thomas, Todd Grant, and Tad Stuelpnagel, who've offered more than they know. Scotty Hightower. Sandra Johnson and Ladette Randolph. All the Zoo poets, especially Joe Osterhaus, Joe Harrison, and Eric Ormsby. The beautiful Jeff Tweedy. And of course the gorgeous Angela Marie Ortiz, for whom this book is offered, may she rest in peace.

# Contents

2
Meditations

# Foreword

The new poet begins with his (dangerously titled) title poem, sited in Shakespeare and likely to lead, or to recede—like most of poetry's post-Homeric transactions with the sea—anywhere, which is not much help to the new reader; it is not for nothing that we are *at sea* when we are lost, trusting merely to what Azevedo calls "the memory of our intentions as the waves come and come and come."

It would seem we are in thrall, as in so much modern poetry, to a grave and testamentary reverence about the treasures of the self as reflected (where else?) in the sea. But right away, in the second line of this emblem piece, the new poet exercises his particular quality, a virtue certainly, though a tormented one, when he observes—casting his nets over his entire production thus far—"as we try to gauge depth, God, still deep, almost talks." Almost! God almost talks! This is a *deus absconditus* indeed, evoked in the second, similarly iconic piece, "From the Hat," by the poet speaking as the mystified performance rabbit:

> . . . the only place
> I still begin to feel—there inside,
> before the lights and faint applause—
> hesitant behind a flash of doves
> in a darkness where I don't exist
> until his hand is there erasing
> the moment when I might not rise.

So much for theology: henceforth we know where we are, and are likely to be—in the hands of an uncertain magician, if not an angry god. . . . There follow, then, invocations to the poet's two sons, and the book's signature piece, the nine "Caspar Hauser Songs," the notes to which remind us that the mysterious victim had been secured to his dungeon floor since birth for sixteen years and had come to accept his fetters as part of his anatomy. The songs follow not a plot nor a narrative, but a sort of visitation:

> Alive in the shaded world of men,
> I knew you as pain, as specific need,
> as the cold thing that was foreign.

Nine "songs," communications on this frantic order, on this stringent disarray: an astonishing poetry, which the entire second half of Azevedo's patiently suffering book (if the pleonasm can stand) attempts to redeem. For such deliverance the poet has access to a sort of demoralized Christian iconography, from which I cite the last three lines of "Three Marys" as an index of the passions [sic] involved:

> He wanted us to weep for someone else,
> but we handle the body beyond speech
> and know the reasons why we hurt ourselves.

A good deal of this religious matter is a mystery, or at least mysterious, but it can remain so without deleting or diminishing the power of the poetry, among the most drastic work of ritual imagination I have encountered in contemporary verse.

And the very strange series concludes with a sort of analogy to all this dark religion, a voice from the natural world, as we like to call it—"The Bearded Seal"—describing an immersion in the native element:

> Three inches in and you begin to feel
> the cold. Heat haunts the sensitive body
> inside your body. Those ghosts reveal
> your underwater breath, your still steady
>
> motion in the dark fragrance of salt.

It seems to me that with these quotations I have provided a kind of evidence an exploring reader of new poetry must have to become a convinced reader of *this* new poetry. It is stark, and it is staked to an unforgiving (or at least *unforgiven*) mode of experience, this work, but it has the tears of things at its heart, and the laughter of ecstasy as well. "The Bearded Seals'" last words upon entering Azevedo's "ocean" are:

> . . . you lie
> to everything that knows and dive. You go
> to the dormant, into that chill, and never die.

—Richard Howard

*The art of our necessities is strange,*
*That can make vile things precious.*
                    —*King Lear,* 3.2.70.

*In the deep bosom of the ocean buried.*
                    —*Richard III,* 1.1.4.

# Ocean

1

# Ocean

This vast unbroken pool spills over our skins, falls still, and
    will not rage.
As we try to gauge depth, God, still deep, almost talks; the
    swimmers slither on and glide.

We remember as we often remember, we enumerate the
    reasons for being here:
the cold Vermeerian color, the blood on our ankles, the
    flavor of salt,

the hidden parting, the cold brine pouring over our cuts, the
    children playing,
the fact of what has happened, kneading and balling the wet,
    dead thought.

The small and varied abrasions bleed down, and in descent
    we see, finally,
our united states spread sleepily among us, hulking,
    hovering, and nearly ready.

As we tread soundlessly over the icy miles, lovelessly, the
    black sounds come,
the memory of blood and our intentions as the waves come
    and come and come

# From the Hat

Perhaps he doesn't know it's not a trick—
each time that I appear, a soft heart
believes, and he is wise. But how I wish
that this could end, wish I could stop
relying on good luck—not to be
the product of a miracle each night,
white complementary to black
inside the hole. It is the only place
I still begin to feel—there inside,
before the lights and faint applause—
hesitant behind a flash of doves
in a darkness where I don't exist
until his hand is there erasing
the moment when I might not rise.

# For Myles

*"Dad, I love you and Mommy—but I <u>like</u> Mommy more."*

I don't like you either, now that you are growing
and can say things as grown-ups
and can prepare cereal by yourself.
The devil has gripped your heart
so that your hands clutch the sill loosely
when you lean out the window.
I don't like your look, your questions
away from a bath, or your bedtime thirst.
Lately, I've been in cahoots
with the monster under your bed.
I don't want you anymore,

so I give you away to your friends
and to tears—to their heat and salt.
Slowly you will stop being a child
and have already stopped listening to my answers,
feeling the breadth of your muscles
living in that health and timber.
Besides, I still have your baby brother,
who springs from the closest of friends,
wanting my arms.
Go away and play with your friends,

my son. I am speaking to you
on a day off in Manhattan,
the trees filling with children,
and their sounds clattering like ice
onto awnings eager to mark a white day
away from the silence of indoors: here:
I am almost thirty and I am suddenly bothered
by your sauntering through perfect snow
giddy in the world's stillness
that is my home for you.

# Owen

My son lies lethargic on my lap,
a sack of heat, a breath that won't collapse,

so flush with flu and so near dry
his skin pouches and he cannot tear,

his tenacious life the ticking to bear—
almost unheard, almost a thing not there,

and invisible as routine: a dropperful
of Pedialyte, a stream of shit,

then a noise that approximates a scream;
what, once revealed, is altered and goes on,

aches as light that penetrates pure eyes,
is less than sleep that simply slips away.

I feel for breath and let him doze because
what can't go on does damage when it does.

# Marco Polo

*A game of hide-and-seek*

Stunned by the blindfold, he is lost
in this front yard suddenly fragrant,

fraught with dark, the bark–hiding moth
deep in alfalfa roiled with gnats,

the hesitations that coil in bats;
his body hedges and prepares for harm

behind the focus of his less familiar eyes;
behind the faithless, fearful, and soft cloth,

feckless, haptic, dazzled, and still,
he works his way through grass filled

blindly by others' passing and their pause
and the giggles as he falls

to stupor, to gesture, to the awful rules.
He flees a sweat bee flanking his ear

and sightlessly searches for all of his choices
until it's clear, and fumbles for their voices.

# Caspar Hauser Songs

## 1. The Dark Lament of His Mouth

Before I was done being born, earthlight
cluttered the floor; small insects fingered my back
and chest, my walls tranquil with the velvet
drape of roots and with cement's cold breath.
In a chain's motion, I heard the mole's thoughts
in darkness lit by my hands. I heard my heart
and the writhing tails of rats. I broke
(as an act of silence) their awful paws,
felt my way into a voice I held
inside my claws, as birds resemble sleep.
That was where I saw my Other—the person
I could please, a fog on the dark glass
nocturnal in reflection, my veiled vessel
to whom I said, *I want to be a horseman.*

## 2. Solitude

And now, a child, there on the floor, quiet
as wood; when smiling, a ceramic bowl,
and ceasing to be or finding myself
still—light dimming my invisible veins.
Always on Advent eve, the horror glass,
sterility of the clock, fingers thrilled
with a fire, the whole world in bed early.
Strange illuminations. From my room,
earth's darkness miles deep. And so it begins
in the auspice of rain, in getting up
from the glass, loosening water, in men,
in their laughter, in memorizing tricks.
This is the silent genius of the deaf—
eyes watering, lips wondering: "Jesus."

## 3. Whiteness

Closer to gods I enter my limp, carefully
step through heaven, where children sully
hot stone, where we keep to ourselves,
most things the burnished pearl of owl's
claw, *snow in siege,* the eyes of community
painless light. Where boys become a human room
for animals to fight; slim breeds,
thin as the thief's hand, as the plum's skin,
bleed. Where those that come closest die.
Then pleasure. Then we speak the language
restive from a throat, wild, an ugly
tongue by which I will consider these
new things (away from the room) you—like my
rat-bloodied hand, like my sacred heart.

## 4. On the Albino Farm . . .

. . . the artisans assume their human shape.
Their practiced claws wake to find my name,
to carve me into fruit, my likeness veiled
beneath the harvest of the field. In heat
the sheets haunt stalks; in their drained skin
they discover winter, scurry for a snow
they plant deep into the color of men.
The specters hear me speak; they listen
for my voice and feed. The demons live
inside my speech and stutter in my throat—
they make me say the things I didn't mean
and search the earth for sound. They sing without
a voice. They wait to live, dissolve to sleep.
They eat. They burn. They harbor all the deaf.

## 5.  First Light

Smoke travels from a burning horse
injured by the dark, then slaughtered.
Flames finger its shape in the field.
Fire, black and swift, cleans the meat off bones
and finds the stud's ash, its final form
loosed over a sodden earth; an odor
veils the bright grass as the moist
scent of char holds my breath to the past.
Scared, I retreat to the familiar,
the deaf light of the rabbit, the speed
from his chalk-covered hands
mimicking movement from where I speak:
a voice hidden inside my mouth,
not dark but lusterless, and deep.

## 6. Der Erlkönig

I see you now, lit by myself: evening's
disguise, color of mist, semblance of vines,
the pleach of clouds swollen with hail.
We touch the ground swiftly; you've shown
me how to hide, to escape in *flight's shadow*.
I see you in the shine of the horse
in hooves moist with alfalfa, slower
in bean spears and in dirt hay-fragrant.
And I follow through the hands of trees
galloping to accept your gifts, Majesty,
with need to be bells warning of frost.
With love, now, show me how to move.
I have come home to lie down in you—
saintlike and febrile at dusk.

## 7. To My Body

It is you they want. We have never been
in love. I'm sorry you've had to be cold,
a handful of lice, animal of my heart.
Where have you been? I shall not
look to worry about what you're about
to do to me in an act of omission.
I will no longer contest your being
heavy and always home. Since you're the wanted,
why not give you to their white hand?
Because as I watch, I want you myself.
How awful that we've grown so attached,
that each betrayal brings my fingers back
to you. For tonight, lie with me: I will
be puncture and breath, and you will like that.

## 8. That the Night Please Us

That's when I woke into the dark white owls,
in medicine. I had become alone.
It was the time before I finished dying,
before I looked for fever in rain,
an illness I could give permission.
Alive in the shaded world of men,
I knew you as pain, as specific need,
as the cold thing that was foreign.
I will always misunderstand the omen,
the obvious image laced in the mind:
all of the life I was not forgetting.
Few appearances are like this. That is why,
ill-lit, I ache as you enter my throat,
rising, a sound in the crowd of the dark.

## 9. *Ich will ein Reiter werden*

The more you see, the more you will return
to me, where nothing is a memory,
where we remember this the same. I am
place: no secret hearth, no oubliette,
just a simple room, a carcass wrapped
in hood: small light, susurrus, and mud.
Hot with fall and shadows on my hair,
my hands lumber onto sand, my knees
release the earth, the grotesque
bulging in the throat, the whole world
coming like a color. As poinsettias
darken by daylight, skin turns heavy
under the douse of sun, the lush and hail
of night: black hurrying hooves.

# Stray

How this man can move my musky hair,
liquored in his slicker and slick chair,
fuzzy and moist in the hand. He is old
in his skin, with fingers that know where
and how to touch. I know what I've been told,
yet how small I grow as I grow scared;
I shiver and feign I do not care
that he is reaching low, he who doesn't care
that I (feeling good now) will not scold
him, having finally learned to mold
myself to men with abandon and a fair
amount of love, to be held while others stare.
Across my teeth I feel the outside's cold
and know I am not home but am not here.

# The Black Angel

Always the impulse to be contained,
a ceaseless impetus beneath the surface

of my lithic stare and feigned sleep.
In a monumental effort not to move

I cling to nightfall, hide my speed from my
belief of bronze. I've risen from a dream

of distance implicit in my form,
a belief that God does not sleep

but watches each dream, each secret hears.
My doubt listens to water seeping.

If only I had been convinced I was
free to rise, regain air, not remain

fixed to what I think of as not wrong,
my awful body sprawled across the dawn.

# Snake

Within your world of glass you are no writher,
your dirty scales disdain electric light
lighting a muscle molded to its cage.
I suspect you breathe, eat, fall asleep,
and never bite, have ceased to find your rage.
I'll go home and pray for your escape
while ripping oranges or shredding grapes,
or perhaps the gentle air of your patience
might come to me in the middle of a stare
I'm caught in and cannot break from,
caught between thought and thought's future,
shimmering with the hum you always hear,
quiet as a shy child knowing something
true: you'd kill me. And I'd kill you.

# Bad Boy

There'll come a time when you must lie
to me about the adult thing that you dared,
and it'll hurt as if you weren't a child,

and there'll be a distance that we'll share
like two Venetian blades of light
separating a bowl of fruit.

Among those shades of shimmering
emptiness we'll come to stare
in other directions—I'll grow unfamiliar

as you become sexual, uncomfortable
in my arms and ever more secret.
I want you to know I know and am prepared

to also retreat into a secret where I am
deceived of you and almost unaware,
a woman one dresses from in daylight,

the woman on the bed grown fat and bare,
ashamed by ugliness, her age,
and the way a boy thinks, and she's partly right

as he becomes half of what she thinks,
a shadow between the table and the door.
The appraisals will be both fair and unfair.

But know I forgive you because you've begun
to dress by yourself and cannot know
how beautiful I always think you are.

# Discarded Nude

I know now where I am
and am afraid. This dark
behind me found me trying

for light from the window.
Could you enter, once again,
what's possible, what you made?

Twenty summers since my face
(am I slightly unattractive
—I mean my wizened nose,

I mean my fading cheek) . . .
I am almost beautiful, too.
Step up to my pale neck.

Is *Still Life with Fruit* done?
Or did you also adumbrate
that dark grape, that soundless bowl?

Come whisper. Slip your touch
across my mess of browns;
wet your fingers, stroke me

with a blush of wine.
Let brushes, soft as lashes,
lift stillness from my flesh:

My hands! Fuck *Self-Portrait*—
his arm cocked into the sun.
At least create my hands.

Where you touched me last,
canvas's gaunt shade. Dry—
a desert I remember

as I remember floods
of color—each rosy scumble
working out my limbs.

See this unshaped thigh?
Your fingers were the wind
when you came close,

hands busy on my skin
industrious across my . . .
This is how I always begin:

no sun, though you make suns,
no child, no world of cyclamen.
I never had a name.

Will White #4
be your pressure on my throat,
my body whisper-still?

I know now where I am.

# New York City

*An homage*

## The Publisher

*For James Raimes*

They are what we quietly acquire,
little habits either bad or good—
but ephemeral, which is why we care
and appear stoic when they disappear.
But the ones one's loved, has tried to insist
on but has come to know one can't protect,
those are the silences of forgotten trysts:
each itself an idea for another,
moving from page to page, never knowing
which is natural. And because we often miss,
we defer to the habit of imagination,
trying to decipher what will not resist and rise
beyond the files to dissipate and die
from what we almost always create: a list.

# The Teacher

*For Richard Howard*

On these couches, I sit, and you read
my poem in this cozy place I come
for lessons—though mostly you just say
what's wrong or right . . . *permissible.*
As I try, you are the saint of language
and, on good days, a walk through WS Park
with Gide. Today you've just retuned
from "turning inertia into muscle mass,"
and I am aware of how heavy I've grown
with all you've said in countless afternoons.
Here beneath David's portrait of you,
a photograph of Proust, and all your reading,
*votre pupille,* I hear everything and become
an angel: invisible, sexless, and dumb.

# The Editor

*For George Plimpton*

The view across the river into Queens
recedes behind the table at which we sit
for dinner. With a ruddy nose you say,
"The proper way to pull the trigger is
between heartbeats," having been on safari,
and all things still fresh in your body
soften your facial features and slim stature
as you retell us about Ernie's eating habits
and 1950s France. I'm warm with the stars
around me, with Scotch and honor's shade
sauntering from your study like a scent
full of ink and paper, leather and liquor,
books and learning from almost every year,
and it's with a shudder (and fear) that I believe.

# The New York Times Morgue

*For Dennis Laurie*

The machinery slows to silence and will
only be disturbed by those recently deceased,
and those of us who have the job of waiting—
just in case—turn down the heat and read.
There is no excitement, nothing grand:
the scent of dust, the hum of microfilm,
the hookers we pass on our way to "lunch,"
the untouched stacks of early runs still warm;
the quiet fidgeting of pigeons on the sill
seems a slow breathing. One grows alone
as the press falls still and cockroaches
crouch in the walls, poised to devour
what remains. My children are home asleep
as gradually the city, like a body, cools.

# Writers

*For Ben, Daniel, David, John, and Max*

One can never understand one's time,
define a moment in a moment, climb
free of temporal existence and see
the making of something meant to be.
One must assume it. And when one does,
it warms one's sense of beauty because
the muse's favor (as you know) is rare
and to witness so many willing to share
stories of her fondling is just good luck
(when one's chosen that certain maid to fuck).
Yet not your friendship but your poetry
is what's at honor here, quality
of a generation safe, and new time
full of the possibility of rhyme.

# Olivia's Belly Button

Inside, the gloomy iguana, the dragon's darkened tongue,
Blood from the princess's torn lip, a wicked riddle,
The fragile failure of an owl's wings and her tiny breath,
The splotchy pink petals reddened with rainwater,
The donkey's heavy laugh, the thrashing of a hundred koi,
All the secrets of little boys, a ghost's dead glow,
A harp's thick heart hearing its own dark song,
An uncontainable smile, four cupcakes, and a tooth,
A garden of tissue flowers, the moist music of an old viola,
Strings and moments made from mercury and moon,
A kitten's mew, sunlight pouring around an eclipse,
A pug's slippery fat kiss, a feather, green from a fern,
A sad giggle, sugar from a Victorian tea party,
The dark light of burning coal, the nothing inside a hole.

# 2

# Meditations

# Supplicium

*Punishment, torment*

. . . and then the silence of a lung.
I could not catch the air, and I hung
on to myself dying into a distance
cut close as blades—my hands' resistance
heavy in the wind. Opening an eye
I saw nothing but light and sky
dripping off my body. I was waking
into my new belief, limbs shaking
with speed and depthless tremors—
I was blind.
                I felt my feathers,
suddenly moist, and an aching chill.
Ice crawled quickly through my stilled
wings. What extinguished all the light
on my body? And then pain, and then heat.

# St. Catherine

*Who recognized Satan in the image of Christ*

It is in God's darkness that I often stare
and always think I see burdens to bear
the dark of, and feelings which I fare
to be human from and somehow freer,
comfortably less clear, yet a little scared
of as I become one in constant glare
focused on the shadows that we share
thickening with that which isn't there,
what each hears and does not hear.
Pray that I find Jesus is not near,
as I, satiated with sin, deny I care,
know a black hand will hold me in either
night. Pray that I do not find forgiveness
in two shades and not feel the difference.

# The Blessed Rafqua Shabaq al-Rayes, the Purple Rose

*Who prayed for pain*

For you He came in spasms of kisses,
blessings of torn skin, and unfettered fevers
for prayers residing in the heat of your hands.
Learning to rest in the spread of your blood,
you avoided the data of the world,
feeling Him in every way you moved,
in blindness and gifts so severe
you ceased to walk. Pray for us stricken
with that other way of suffering, an infliction
of our own intent, our own humid scent
emanating from our flesh, how we obey
the spirits we think are not pain but are beyond
the pain we seek; pray we learn to hurt
what can neither give nor receive comfort.

# St. Dymphna

*Who intercedes for the possessed and insane*

We think of comfort as constructed simply,
an architecture of altar and tabernacle,
the place to hope for disasters when able
to engage in instinct beyond our decisions
we chose or didn't choose, an illness
we didn't avoid by standing in the rain—
the droplets tracing our necks and elbows,
attempting the artificial and sane,
the plain way of being able to resume
the graceless station of staying intent
on the natural impulse and its aching.
Hear us, Dymphna, as we become possessed
and stilled by all we would invent by being
icy, incoherent, and completely content.

# St. Maria-Goretti

*Who prayed for death instead of rape*

He turned his face away and hid, hid
in the darkest shadows of my face,
subverted the impulse to be mercy
and forced belief you wouldn't be missed,
clothed you in the raiment of his kisses.
He prayed but did not imagine hell.
I find myself inside the human race:
a constant sound to which my heart responds,
is not fond of, the craft that has contained
your frame of youth, your return to me,
your forgiveness and my concession.
Maria, pray for me now, for a reverence
I would have you understand:
my sincerest love, my simplest shame.

# St. Mary Magdalene

*Who was loved by Jesus*

Perhaps there *are* two of us, dear Mary,
waiting in wonder before the well,
in something less than ecstasy, kneeling
and almost knowing why. Perhaps by feeling
not forgiveness but anguish, dousing our hair
as a cloth, scenting the innocent bare
feet, we come to care for the naked skin
we are denied and are pardoned by frustrating
the evil that exists in loving our friends.
It's certain we should shed the shadows
we've acquired, but in what impulse of oblation?
Which presence should we prefer and why?
With everything revealed, show us prostration:
Which is false? To which should we aspire?

# Witness

*A passion*

## 1. A Boy

Maybe it wasn't I who ran away,
young and surrounded by men,
sincerely hidden but unable to abide
being outside his ken. I watched to see
the way, difficult to see the band
moving back over the way we came,
tried keeping pace with all of them.
So many left when he was silenced
and led down, but I strayed on, faithful,
following from shadow to shadow,
lasting past a burgeoning neglect,
advent of cerements. Beyond the gray
I vanished but managed to hang on, and
until one reached out, I did not run away.

## 2. Malchus

I know the damage lucky blows can deal,
part of me severed in the dark outside
the garden; my scream revealed my blood,
and that crowd watched me shrink in shame.
I could not rise, at least run away,
and knelt for the help of his right hand.
Better it had lain there in the sand, better
to have avoided my miracle and moved on.
His group grew afraid as they dispersed,
as his fingers disappeared from trauma,
from our entire wish, and all of us unhealed.
How I crave he'd left me all alone
and stayed a coward (with his stability,
his worn face) watching us. So many wounds.

## 3. Annas

*To Caiaphas*

This man's Hebrew? Then he must be
informed of that and feel God in his heart
(we well know how that can sting)
and of the things Antipas won't forgive,
a slander or a misplaced name. This one's
words could someday return to him. . . .
See he keeps the Sabbath, regards our place,
and is mindful of God's order. And he must pray.
We've often said that most mistakes occur
from being either unaware or too faithful.
Remember, one can be *almost* right, and
remember how he's certain and persuades
(and so far removed from, yet so similar)
about our mystery. Show him our way.

## 4. Barabbas

*A Zealot's prayer*

I've done more for you than most.
As I erase the dark across my heart,
I've lost loyalty to those for whom I fought,
to what my hands almost contained. And while
I struggle in man's fingers, my voice
and strength have helped so little,
if at all. I see the reasons why I failed
and am now afraid to die. I don't want
to fall asleep yet, in bonds I feel
the Roman deepening around me:
give me what I still need to fight, believe
the Messiah will murder this enemy,
to give my life and, more, to wait
for the moment in which I might escape.

## 5. From the Crowd

We must expect the one of whom we've heard
to really come now, rising from God's sleep
when everything will happen for the first time
and our children will not remember
chaos risen from many a charismatic mouth.
We must invent our own secret evening
full of spring, our own collective power.
Goodness must be preserved, and it is good
because we cannot stop those who fear
why we must wait. Now, we must create
public opinion, gather in our throat
voices of our fathers now grown faint,
our tradition of saying what we say
in our belief and disbelief: Crucify him!

## 6. A Soldier

I have tried to be careful, delicate,
and had to go to several different spots
before I found stems ripe enough to wrap
and long enough to twine. Some tracks
across my arms will surely scar, the blood
still running from deeper cuts. My fingertips,
almost numb, are throbbing, tender vines,
wet thorns stuck inside my nails,
my lips torn by tying the final knot.
I have given this work my best attention
because it wasn't enough just to detain;
the pain has been excessive and seemed rough.
I don't like to complain, but now he's gowned,
the crown must fit, so press it down!

## 7. Pontius Pilate

As we emerged out onto the pavement,
I could hear the mob, fervent for frailty,
feel its way toward us. We were each alone.
To divert its attention is always best, to calm;
yet this time I would distort its motive
and its claim on him. Such was my dignity.
But I wrongly gauged my powers to persuade
and saw my words swallowed with his mouth.
Still, I tried having slowed it by dressing him
to calm its taste—until it revealed its maw
and its dull voice. I let go. If only I hadn't
been so similar to something weakened,
displayed before the image of my hid belief,
chosen but useless. We were both forsaken.

## 8. Judas Iscariot

Suddenly I possessed his suffering and calm,
could solve the impotence of blind devotion,
and I understood possession's real relief.
I held a morsel of his power. I could kiss
on equal terms. I could love, invested
by knowledge of what we didn't know.
But the horror of remembering my innocence,
for which I grieve and will not let myself
forget. Unlike others I owned my doubt,
owed a mouth of blood, and was not
deceived. For he had no right to speak
my curse in his vague effective way—
a destiny he noticed without fear or force.
How it hurt to realize it was I.

## 9. Simon of Cyrene

We're already growing less creative
as we strive to lighten the trying, try
only to be blessed, and with our lives
we'll shy sightlessly from that light.
We're trying not to see our possibility—
if we were birds we'd not be flying—
the act of inertia before us
to carry the splinters of our human heart.
We're falling, the sunlight in our eyes;
earthly, we're trying to rise again,
realizing we've fewer things to decide.
We're tired of striving not to trust
our need to rest in the fine soft dirt,
and in this way we keep ourselves alive.

## 10.  Peter

For my conviction I'm prepared to die,
am often moved to repeat fidelity,
am single in my thought, will remember
how I propose to act and not devote
a single smile to the impulse to desert
hours of attention, lessons taught,
to miscomprehend or not to speak.
I've not been giving in to inaccuracy
but, in others, haven't been unforgiving.
I will emerge into my new habits,
a flash from another's face and frame,
for whom, unready, I promised to forget
my name, promised not to fail or flee.
Under punishment of tears I send myself
to reaffirm my speech: *I am your friend.*

## 11. Gestas

The growing need to see another light
rise consumes my sight, and so I clutch
an empty hand full of iron. Evening
swells against my broken thigh, dense.
They are finally dead, as I must be
before they'll take me down. In darkness
now, the women have stopped crying.
They have become the touch of rain;
one who's seen my heavy body hang,
who looks and needs to take me down
and to her house in a town close by,
attempts to heal my hands, wipe wrists,
press my eyes against the dark of her
that's me, hearing her say it's not yet time.

## 12. Three Marys

Though he understood each thing has a voice
that argues with the way it comes across—
the thing that is with the way we speak;
though he understood we'd turn back
into ourselves, keep our love, and cry for him;
though he knew our need to stay and kneel
and *not* believe for a while, our need
after he cleansed us of excessive love,
we admit we can't accept a cadaver razed
to bone, and we hold each pain, each rip
deep in our mouths and in our sleep.
He wanted us to weep for someone else,
but we handle the body beyond speech
and know the reasons why we hurt ourselves.

## 13. Joseph of Arimathea

To be the first to hold him in my arms,
to linger on him while he has to rest,
to repair wounds and his torn skin,
to confirm his shattered person into place,
to hear a stillness haunt and leave his lips,
to see for certain that he finally sleeps,
to feel alone and everything I've felt,
to please him as I please and not be seen,
to bury evidence of his defeat,
to hide in tombs in these fresh hours,
to free myself from thoughts I have to shun,
to crave a quiet that will devour love,
to understand why only I believe,
to cover all the damage I have done.

## 14. Nicodemus

As I see the remains, I believe its parts,
as I prepare its presence and final place
praying against the rigidity, as I
confirm each cut and document his death,
I anoint with balm and Jewish rite.
*How can these things be,* our poverty
displayed among his torso, head, and palms?
I'm healing when it's too late to forgive,
cowering in psalms I've tried to live,
as the cold harrows the skin, the linen
bloodless and dry and beautifully stitched.
In midnight's pattern I've come to believe
in how to keep his image fresh and here
while we suffer. While he needs to sleep.

# On Being Jesus' Age at Death

Approaching the end of my thirty-third year
I am not wise and often suffer, fear
I've abandoned my children, want to kill
myself like my lover, an involuntary act of will-
fullness. I, too, am ready to empty my breath
but can't inflict a deliberate death
my children will know of and someday suffer.
If only to grow sick and not get better,
trick You into (thinking?) that I slipped
into traffic, or lost all my blood while I slept.
Though, I find it difficult to imagine my will
so confused as to want to kill
me, the one, that brought my daughter fear
and my death in my young thirty-third year.

# Marana Tha

*Come, Lord*

I'm tired, and I want to rest a minute here
underneath the covers and warm clothes,
comfortable in a moment of no future beer.
The bearably precise way I will repose
both now and days from now comforts me
in the heated afternoon, unshowered
and prickly with stubble and stale sweat, free,
for a moment, of the funereal flowers
long since desiccated. I can barely move
as the sun travels over my hairy belly,
beard, and hot bed. I've nothing now to lose,
and the emptying left me warm and smelly;
so I suspect I'll lie here—limp and alive—
in habit in case someone should arrive.

# Anastasis

*The harrowing of hell*

The sun that soaked up all the hours
is being lowered into a starved flower
that, on the verge of powder, feels wild,
having abandoned hope for a cool shower,
and appears like the severed hand of a child:
cold as a leaf, unsmooth with power,
not fast breaths or water-bright, and sour—
the calyx cuplike, brown, brittle, and mild.
Night began to finger out the damaging light,
windless air grew less warm, and glow
diminished, defiled daylight, and dispersed.
When the dark grew familiar and felt right
and the embers warmed each extremity below,
it rejected comfort and reveled now immersed.

# Animi Cruciatus

*Affliction of spirit*

Imagine the bullet cracking her skull,
entering the frontal lobe, the blood
under her face like a halo, the flood
of her final breath, inhaled and exhaled, full
of peppermint and smoke, or her head
pressing down on her warm, wet hair.
There is no peace in the sound of a prayer,
just as there is no sound in the dead
silence of an eyelid or leg muscle
at three-thirty-six in the morning;
that's the repetitive language of sin,
not surrendering in sweat and hustle,
movement attempting to hide all warning,
a ritual peculiar to angels and to man.

# Compunctio Cordis

*Repentance of heart*

Things are still snow.
I see evening in a mist of gulls,
their orange bellies swarming
as my balance comes, shallow
as shadow drawn from the color blue.
What is contained in a blessing?
I imagine its dream of escape,
its way of opening.
The night opens for snow
and mirrors light from the town.
I'm searching for an area of sun,
tickled by the deep shine that keeps me
to the blue memory of pain not mine.
You've forgotten how to comfort me.

# The Bearded Seal

Three inches in and you begin to feel
the cold. Heat haunts the sensitive body
inside your body. Those ghosts reveal
your underwater breath, your still, steady

motion in the dark fragrance of salt.
Grains of ice float off your whiskers
and rise lightly through ocean's nudge and halt
of light and dark, of water's tons: the askers

of you: a mute, a steady wing. A question
they follow now, you seem to hate the sea,
and seem to be the bear's reflection
that ghosts the mirror's thought, banality

and shadow that's a larger thought of you
now swimming through the world turned white:
white predators, the weather white, the food
a darkness to avoid. From color you invite

the universe, and, watching from the floe,
a monk, the largest brown of depth, you lie
to everything that knows and dive. You go
to the dormant, into that chill, and never die.

# Notes

"Caspar Hauser Songs": Before being found on the street in Nuremberg, Germany, barely able to walk or speak at the age of sixteen, Caspar Hauser had been secured since birth to the floor of an underground dungeon, which he, as he says in his eight-page autobiography, "accepted as part of his anatomy." He became a subject of study for German intellectuals, evidence, they imagined, of a tabula rasa, their own wolf-child. He enjoyed the attention and received an education. Three years later an unknown assailant murdered him as mysteriously as he appeared. "The Dark Lament of His Mouth" is from Georg Trakl's poem "Caspar Hauser Lied" (*Lied* being German for *song*). "Snow in Siege" is from *Paradise Lost,* book 9. "Der Erlkönig," translated literally, is "The Elf King" and is taken from Goethe's poem of that title. The final title, "*Ich will ein Reiter werden,*" translates as "I want to be a horseman," again from Trakl. Though historical in subject, the poem is informed by experiences gathered in St. Joseph's Center for Mental Health in 1989.

"Witness": 'A Boy,' Mark 14:52; 'Malchus,' John 18:10; 'Annas,' John 18:24; 'Barabbas,' Mark 15:7; 'From the Crowd,' Mark 15:8; 'A Soldier,' Matthew 27:27–29; 'Pontius Pilate,' John 18:38; 'Judas Iscariot,' Luke 22:3; 'Simon of Cyrene,' Mark 15:21; 'Peter,' Luke 22:62; 'Gestas,' Matthew 27:44–45; 'Three Marys,' John 19:26; 'Joseph of Arimathea,' Luke 23:53; 'Nicodemus,' John 19:39–40.